WILDERNESS
of
AMERICA

CLB 1784
© 1987 Colour Library Books Ltd., Guildford, Surrey, England.
Printed and bound in Barcelona, Spain by Cronion, S.A.
All rights reserved.
Published 1987 by Portland House, distributed by Crown Publishers, Inc.
ISBN 0 517 63115 6
hgfedcba

WILDERNESS
of
AMERICA

Text by
BILL HARRIS

PORTLAND HOUSE

Back in 1940, the essayist E.B. White took a trip to Concord, Massachusetts to have a look at Walden Pond, where Henry David Thoreau retreated in 1845 to get back to nature and to protest the increasing assaults on the wilderness that he perceived to be reaching epidemic proportions.

Thoreau's retreat resulted in a book that made the man famous. White's visit resulted in an essay in the form of a letter to the naturalist. He pointed out that finding the pond had become much easier in the mid-20th century: just turn left at the Minuteman Chevrolet Company, pass the Golden Pheasant Lunchroom and when you reach the campground called Walden Breezes, you are practically there.

"Behind the Breezes, in a sun-parched clearing, dwelt your philosophical descendants in their trailers ... all grouped together for the sake of congeniality," White's letter said. "... A few flies came out to greet me and convoy me to your cove, past the No Bathing signs on which the fellows and the girls had scrawled their names." He continued, "I felt strangely excited suddenly to be snooping around your premises tiptoeing around watchfully, as though not to tread by mistake upon the intervening century. Before I got to the cove, I heard something which seemed to me quite wonderful: I heard your frog, a full, clear *troonk*, guiding me, still hoarse and solemn. But he soon quit and I came upon a group of small boys throwing stones at him.

"... There were the remains of a fire in your ruins, but I doubt it was yours; also two beer bottles trodden into the soil and become part of the earth. A young oak had taken root in your house, and two or three ferns, unrolling like ticklers at a banquet. The only other furnishings were a DuBarry pattern sheet, a page torn from a picture magazine, and some crusts in wax paper."

It's easy to nod in agreement with E.B. White's letter to Thoreau and to give a rueful shake of your head at America's seeming lack of caring for the gifts of nature. But compared to the 1980s, the American wilderness in the 1940s was positively primitive. Automobiles seldom went more than 50 miles an hour, there were few highway interchanges and the concrete spaghetti they would serve was still a long way in the future. Most Americans stayed in cities and towns except for the first two weeks in August, and the bulldozer was still in its early development stage.

Yet if we seem to have spent the last few centuries trying to destroy Wilderness America, there is strong evidence we have failed.

The fact is that no one since the Stone Age has ever seen the North American continent in a natural state untouched by man. As soon as the first Indians crossed the land bridge over the Bering Sea, the forest primeval ceased to exist. They hacked their way across the continent with stone axes, criss-crossed the forests and grasslands with wide trails, and from the very beginning were almost single-minded about setting fires to drive out game or to clear land for farms and settlements. The Europeans brought new technology to the job but they didn't invent the game.

By 1700, George Washington wrote, "Our lands were originally very good, but use and abuse have made them quite otherwise. We ruin the lands that are already cleared, and either cut down more wood, if we have it, or emigrate to the Western country." At that point the band of settlement along the Eastern seaboard didn't extend inland for more than 100 miles. A little more than a century later, a third of all Americans lived west of the Appalachian Mountains. And they were all working furiously to change the landscape. They were so successful, in fact, that in less than another 100 years they had managed to destroy more than two-thirds of the timber that was standing in the United States the day the Pilgrims first set foot on Plymouth Rock.

Interestingly, when the first settlers crossed the mountains into what is now Ohio and Indiana, they found changes in the wilderness that had been made by one of the legendary figures of early America. His name was John Chapman. When he died in the 1830s, his obituary in an Indiana newspaper identified him as a "nurseryman."

To call Johnny Appleseed a nurseryman is about the same as calling George Washington a "planter." He wandered through the wilderness for more than 50 years planting apple trees as well as other fruits and medicinal plants he knew would be useful to the settlers who would follow in his footsteps.

He began his wanderings in Pittsburg, after having planted orchards all the way from Massachusetts to Pennsylvania. Everyone who knew him loved him, even the Indians who were generally hostile to the white man. But even those who loved him most had to admit he cut a rather bizarre figure. They say he wore a coffee sack with cut-out armholes as a shirt and a stewing kettle passed for a hat. He always walked barefoot, even in winter, and had an uncanny knack for finding his way anywhere without a map or compass. He would appear quietly and mysteriously at the doors of settlers' cabins to ask for a place to spend the night. When he was welcomed inside, he always refused to sleep anywhere but on the floor, and before the sun rose in the morning he had vanished as mysteriously as he had appeared the evening before.

Johnny was deeply religious and led an utterly selfless life. He didn't own a gun and found it impossible to hurt any living thing. One story about him says he once doused the flames of his campfire so the mosquitoes wouldn't be burned to death. He never ate meat, and would never accept anything from anyone unless he could exchange it for seeds or a small tree.

For years after he died, people on the frontier exchanged stories about this wonderful little man. And they loved him so much that almost none of them ever touched a tree he had planted, except to harvest the fruit. They were about the only trees they didn't touch.

In New England and south to Virginia, they had completely eliminated the pine and hemlock forests and the dominant trees became maples, oaks and birches. In the midwest, whole forests were leveled, leaving grasslands that even today mark the landscape in Michigan and Wisconsin. Plants and species of birds that were once limited to the open prairie moved east as man moved west. And if opening the forest cover to encourage deciduous trees gave the East more spectacular autumn colors, making the environment attractive to prairie ragweed took away a lot of the pleasure.

On the other hand, thanks to the hand of man, the vast pine forests of the South, once levelled to make way for more profitable cotton and tobacco plantations, have been restored, and in the process animals that once lived there have been able to go home again. There are more deer in American forests right now than were there before the white man came. And though the search for beaver and otter made exploration of the West profitable, neither animal is on the endangered species list any longer. The beaver, in

fact, goes right on cutting trees and damming streams and altering the landscape of the wilderness that has been spared.

The first Europeans who saw the North American continent were more impressed by its seacoasts than by its wilderness. The interior was a barrier to the riches they were sure lay beyond. Vasco Nunez de Balboa was the first to range inland when he trekked across the Central American jungle in 1513 and concluded that the continent was only about 50 miles wide. But it was a hellish 50 miles, and nobody cared to follow in his footsteps. The coast itself was enough of a challege to the likes of John Cabot, who claimed North America for England; to his son Sebastian, who explored the claim from Newfoundland to Cape Hatteras; to Giovanni da Verrazano, who explored the same 1500 miles of coastline 25 years later and claimed it for the King of France. When Verrazano saw Pamlico Sound from Cape Hatteras, he was excited by the fact that Balboa's Western Sea seemed to be only about a mile away. But he never bothered to check.

And so it went for more than 200 years. The great American wilderness was there for anyone to see, but the waterborne explorers chose not to deal with it. The coast was good enough for them. And what a varied seacoast it is. Between Northern Canada and Cape Cod, it is rocky, wild and cold. South of Boston harbor, the landscape begins to soften and the rocks are laced with sandy beaches, which soon take over completely and stretch almost all the way down to the southern end of Florida, where another form of rock takes over again in the coral-based Florida Keys. Centuries after Balboa discovered the Pacific Ocean, other explorers would sail up the continent's west coast and report an almost impenetrable wall of rocky cliffs along its entire length.

The continent between is somewhat like a basin, with the Appalachian Mountains on the eastern rim and the Pacific Coast Range on the west. On the Atlantic coast, the continental shelf extends about a hundred miles out to sea, which is why the coastline is gentler. In the Pacific, the shelf drops as dramatically off the shore as the cliffs rise above it. But for all the drama of its coasts, the diversity of the American wilderness is unique in all the world. From top to bottom, North America spans latitudes ranging from polar to tropic. It has mountains of every size, areas where rain almost never falls and places where it never seems to stop. It has soil ranging from sand to clay to hardscrabble to lushly fertile.

Before man began changing the landscape, a great green forest almost entirely covered the eastern half of the continent as far west as the Mississippi River, north to the Dakotas and south into Texas. North from the Great Lakes, the forest was mostly hardwoods and hemlocks, giving way eventually to deciduous trees and then to the pine woods of the coastal south. The grassy prairie took over near the Mississippi River and the forests began again with the rise of the Rocky Mountains, where spruce, fir and pine abounded. Beyond the mountains a forbidding desert stretched on toward the Sierra Nevada and the Cascades, where the moisture from the coast encouraged the giant sequoias in the south and the towering Douglas fir, spruce, cedar and hemlock in the rainy northwest.

It was all there when Balboa hacked his way across the Central American jungle, but no European even dreamed of it. And although great stretches of the original wilderness have since been lost forever, what remains is still one of the natural wonders of the world. And, fortunately, vast stretches of it are being protected for the future.

The biggest and richest wilderness anywhere on earth is also one of the world's great population centers. It is known to scientists as the "Oak-Deer-Maple Biome," but the term "green woods" suits it better. It is a forest that still extends across the Great Lakes region and south to the Gulf of Mexico. It covers part of Florida and extends west to the Ozark Mountains.

It has been estimated that only slightly less than one tenth of one percent of that forest has never been touched by man. Almost all the native animals have been driven out as well, but some have returned. Moose have been spotted in upstate New York and mountain lions still roam in Northern Pennsylvania. But the greatest change of all takes place each and every year, when the trees get their new leaves in the spring. The entire forest becomes brand new. The sun warms the ground, which will in a few short weeks become shady and cool. Flowers bloom everywhere and birds and small animals are busy building new homes.

Other forests in other parts of the world, even in other parts of North America, have more dramatic growth and more colorful birds and animals, but none has the variety of wildlife and as many different kinds of trees as the wilderness of the East, which in spite of highways and parking lots, sprawling cities and towns, still has all the earmarks of a wilderness.

The forest covers the entire eastern third of the continent, and though it has been dramatically altered, nature has protected her own, and no one in the Eastern United States is ever far from a rewarding walk in the woods. And what an experience it is! Anyone who has ever heard the whisper of a breeze in the high branches, or been startled by an equally startled pheasant in the tall grass, or watched a squirrel run across the uneven top of a stone wall, has come away from the experience untouched. Anyone who has ever felt compelled to stop breathing for a moment or two so as not to frighten a pair of grazing deer never forgets those breathless moments.

In the spring, there is a special pleasure in discovering a marsh filled with marigolds and hearing the song of a robin for the first time in months. And has any painter ever quite been able to catch the soft green of the first willow buds? Or the red tinges on a skunk cabbage leaf? They're all fleeting pleasures and a painter trying to catch those colors had better be quick about it because once the show starts, it moves as quickly as a circus performance. The birds have no sooner begun to build their nests than the willow leaves darken, other trees burst their buds, and the lilies are replaced by dogwood and violets. Then, as the days grow warmer, the new leaves get less shiny, the flowers less bright. Squirrels get busy cleaning up and burying the fruit and nuts that drop from the trees by day, and and at night raccoons come out to see what they've left behind. Every creature in every pocket of the forest seems to have a job to do and every one of them seems to have the impression that it must be done right then and there.

They may be right. As every schoolboy knows, summer is the shortest time of the year, and in parts of the woodlands of the northeast the prime of life can be as short as a dozen weeks. But, like the final movement of a great symphony, it ends with a spectacle. The drama begins on a chilly September night up above the Bay of Fundy and in a month or so extends all the way down into the Great Smoky Mountains. It is called autumn. In the northeast they call it wonderful. It all happens because of a very simple chemical reaction. When the temperature drops below 45 degrees, the cells in the structure of the leaves of trees tighten, cutting off the production of green chlorophyll and causing a reaction with the sugars that have accumulated in the tree over the summer, making them turn to red, scarlet, yellow and dozens of other spectacular colors. The arrival of fall brings longer nights, and that's when the work is done, but it is at its best by day when the bright sunshine heightens the colors.

Each species turns a different color. Poplars and birches turn lemon yellow, dogwood, mountain ash and burberry become rich red. If a tree is brownish red it is probably a beech, and if it is rich brown it is an oak. But, fortunately for those of us who rearrange our schedules to be near the forest in the early weeks of October, the one tree that changes to a variety of colors is also the most common. Depending on its type, a maple tree can become bright red, scarlet or brilliant yellow or, as if to add interest, it might stay green.

The spectacle doesn't last more than a week or two before all the colorful leaves are on the ground, enriching it for next year's performance, the groundhogs are snug in their burrows waiting for February 2, when they'll come out to make their annual prediction about the arrival of spring, and the ducks and geese are high-tailing it for warmer waters. But during that time, millions of people from Boston to Washington will have been able to see the show without venturing more than a few miles from their front doors, and not one of them will think they have been anywhere near the American wilderness.

The place most likely to get their vote as Wilderness America could well be the mountains of the West. Though most Easterners think that every mountain from mid-Colorado west to the Pacific is part of the Rockies, the mountains that mark the Continental Divide are only about100 miles wide in many places and they never extend from east to west for more than 500 miles. But they are part of the longest mountain chain in the world, extending 10,000 miles from Alaska to Patagonia. They are the dominant feature in six of the United states and two Canadian provinces. In Colorado alone, more than 50 peaks rise to altitudes of more than 14,000 feet, compared to only 11 such peaks in Switzerland, and 1,500 are more than 10,000 feet high.

There are more than 4,500 species of plants and trees native to the Rocky Mountains, and hundreds of different animals, from gophers to grizzly bears. Where they live depends on a variety of factors, from altitude to availability of water. Below 6,000 feet, the vegetation is likely to be short grasses and stunted trees. Going up to 10,000 feet, ponderosa pine shares the territory with willows, birches, aspen and alders. Blue spruce grows near the streams and, in dryer areas, pinon pine and juniper. The next thousand feet is known as the Subalpine Zone. Both the air and the soil are thinner there and the pines give way to hardier spruces and carpets of wildflowers. The "tree line" begins at about 11,500 feet and the Alpine slopes above it are covered with flowering plants. The line is never an even division because trees can grow in sheltered places, but every high peak is eventually crowned in summer with a halo of flowers.

Animals and birds have their own territories, too, though deer and coyotes, marmots and chipmunks, among others, live at every altitude. The highest meadows are the year-round home of such creatures as the ptarmigan and rosy finch, who are joined in summer by bighorn sheep, elk and others who spend the colder months further down the slopes. The Subalpine Zone is the range of the bobcat and a dozen varieties of birds, and below that is where the deer and the antelope play.

Americans have their own wilderness playgrounds in the Rockies in the five National Parks that cover almost four million acres of preserved wilderness. There are also millions of acres protected by the Forest Service, most of which include recreational facilities. The best-known of the Rocky Mountain parks is also the oldest in the world, and the biggest in the United States. The more than two million acres of Yellowstone National Park and the eight million acres of National Forest that surround it are visited each year by more people than live in the three states that contain them. But in spite of the presence of all those cars and campers, in spite of the modern hotel facilities, cafeterias and convenience stores, the wilderness experience is there, and it is possible to spend days on end in parts of the park without seeing another human being.

There are plenty of other things to see in Yellowstone. There are 165 rushing streams with inspiring cataracts and waterfalls. There are 36 lakes, covering 165 square miles. There are hills and valleys, canyons and mountain peaks. There are hundreds of species of wildlife, from meadow mice to moose. There are herds of buffalo, bands of bighorn sheep, families of elk, deer and antelope and packs of coyotes. And no visitor to Yellowstone can go anywhere without being approached, gingerly, of course, by a begging chipmunk. In the fall, eagles fly north to feed on salmon, which have made the trip the hard way. They often compete with ospreys for the same morsels, and the thousands of ducks carefully stay out of their way. There are swans and cranes, even pelicans and seagulls, on the lakes. There are hawks and meadowlarks, hummingbirds and herons and, forever changing the landscape, incredibly busy beavers.

For all that activity, the one thing visitors ask each other when they get back to the motels in West Yellowstone each night is "Did you see any bears?" Occasionally the answer is yes, but most often they have to content themselves with the innkeeper's tales of multiple sightings last week, last month or last spring. And they go out the next morning to look some more along the park's 500 miles of paved roads or 1,000 miles of marked trails. Finding wildlife is easy along the roads. All you need to do is look for the backed-up cars. Park regulars call them "moosejams." But finding bears? It happens every day. It just never seems to happen at the right time for most vacationers.

The passion for seeing bears in Yellowstone began back in the 1920s, when a big black bear decided to take a nap in the middle of the Grand Loop Road. A sightseeing bus came along and no amount of horn-blowing could get the beast to wake up. One of the passengers solved the problem by tossing a sandwich out the window. The bear gulped it down and let the bus pass. The next morning when the tour went through, there was the bear again. After a few days, when it seemed that the animal had memorized the bus schedule, it became a regular part of the tour and, as word got around, the most popular part. Over the years, as visitors became more aggressive, many of the black bears were rounded up and moved into the interior. The moves were said to be protective measures because, for all its cute and cuddly appearance, a 300-pound bear can do a lot of damage. But the protection works both ways and the relocation program has probably saved more bears than people, because in past decades bears who displayed the slightest antisocial tendencies were simply shot.

Black bears symbolize the Yellowstone wilderness, but they share equal billing with some

10,000 geysers, hot springs and mud volcanoes that are among the unique geothermal features forming a basin 30 miles wide and 50 miles deep across the center of the park. They are the remnants of ancient volcanoes that were active about 50 million years ago and haven't run out of steam yet. The Indians generally avoided the place, and white men didn't arrive to explore it until 1807, when John Colter, a scout on the Lewis and Clark Expedition, detached himself from the party on their way back from Oregon and spent the next four years exploring the Rocky Mountains. When he finally got back to Saint Louis and described what he had seen, nobody believed him. But even if it was a tall tale, it was a memorable one, and the territory he explored became known as "Colter's Hell."

As far as John Colter was concerned, his experience in the Rocky Mountain wilderness was as close to the gates of hell as any man would ever want to be, and geysers had nothing to do with it. He hadn't been exploring long when he met a trader named Manuel Lisa, who hired him to go find some Indians and convince them they should become customers of the white man's trading post.

One of Colter's biographers wrote "… this man with a pack of thirty pound weight, his gun and some ammunition went upward of 500 miles to the Crow nation, gave them information and proceeded thence to several other tribes."

It wasn't nearly that simple. At one point, when he was on his way to drum up business at Pierre's Hole, just west of Teton Pass, the party of Crows he was traveling with was attacked by Blackfeet. The Crows were good prospects as customers so Colter helped them out. In the process he was wounded in the leg, but helped save his companions from defeat. That didn't sit too well with the Blackfeet, who felt humiliated by having been beaten by a paleface. That, combined with his leg wound, made Colter anxious to get back to the safety of Lisa's fort. He headed north alone and, according to the story, went directly across the territory that is Yellowstone Park today.

It is a fact that he made it back to the fort safely. And when he did, Lisa gave him a promotion. He was no longer a traveling salesman, but became a trapper.

One morning when he and a companion were out checking their traps, they heard rustling noises along a river bank. Convincing themselves it was just a herd of buffalo down for a drink, they pressed on. They were sorry they did when a party of Blackfeet in warpaint appeared on the shore. There was no avenue of escape, so the white men did what they thought was expected of them when the chief motioned them ashore. As Colter's friend's canoe touched the bank, one of the Indians reached out and took his gun away from him. Colter rushed over, grabbed the gun back and gave it to the other white man who, apparently confused, pushed his canoe back into the river. He took an arrow in the leg for that.

Realizing that his wound made any hope of escape impossible, he picked up his gun and killed one of the Blackfeet. Their response was to riddle his body with bullets. That left Colter all alone in the hands of a lot of very angry Blackfeet. They were especially irritated over the fact that the white man had died so quickly. That was no fun at all for these people, who were very inventive about making the death of their enemies very slow and very painful. But the good news for them was that they still had a live enemy to deal with. They held a council to decide what to do about it, and after a long deliberation announced they would strip him naked and let him run for his life.

John Colter was no cream puff, but the territory the Indians had in mind for him to run through was strewn with sharp stones and tough underbrush. The Indians were so sure he wouldn't get very far without shoes, they gave him a hundred-yard head-start before they started howling after him. And why not? It was fully five miles to the nearest cover and they didn't want to tear him to pieces until he'd had a little time to think about it.

He had run about three miles when he dared to turn his head to see how near death might be. And, wonder of wonders, only one Indian was anywhere near. Slowing down, he called back over his shoulder asking the brave to spare him. But the Indian would have none of that. Instead, he lunged forward with his spear tightly clenched in both hands. Fortunately, the long run had tired him, too, and Colter was able to grab the spear before it hit its mark. The head of the spear broke off in his hands, and Colter used it to kill the Blackfoot brave.

By then the rest of the band was gaining on him and they were more furious than ever, having watched one of their brothers die at the hands of a naked white man. Colter sprinted the rest of the way to a river bank and its protective cover of trees. In the middle of the river he spotted a beaver lodge. As a trapper, he knew the habits of beavers and was well aware that their lodges were built with no entrances except under water. He also knew that there was plenty of room inside for a man to be quite comfortable, as long as he didn't mind not standing up. Without pausing to think about all that, he jumped into the river, quickly found the underwater entrance to the beaver lodge and was sitting high and dry inside when the Indians arrived.

They looked everywhere for him. And even though they, too, must have known about the construction of beaver lodges, it never dawned on them that an ordinary white man could be that attuned to the mysteries of nature. Before long, they concluded that he must still be running and took off in the most likely direction.

Colter stayed put and it was lucky he did, because in a couple of hours the Blackfeet came back to poke around some more. They left quickly, muttering angrily to themselves. By the time the sun went down, Colter figured it was safe enough to come out of hiding. He was far from safe, of course, and he knew it. Armed with just the broken spearhead, he began a long trek back to civilization. Fearful of Indians, he opted for the tough route, straight up and over the mountains. It took him more than ten days to make it back to the fort.

Later when he told the tale he said he was no worse for the adventure than a little sunburn and sore feet. It's because of things like that that no one believed his tales of geysers and mud volcanoes. But the people who welcomed him back to Lisa's fort knew this particular tale was at least mostly true. He was in such bad shape no one recognized him.

Any other man probably would have gone back East after an adventure like that, but John Colter had a line of traps to tend. On the theory that the Blackfeet would leave the mountains for the winter, he began his next trip away from the fort after the first snow had fallen. His theory was wrong. He was attacked at the edge of the Continental Divide, narrowly escaped again, and once again was forced to cross the mountains the hard way. The following spring he went back to Saint Louis. He died there, quietly, a few years later.

Mountain men like John Colter had much more to be concerned about than hostile Indians. Their adventures with an untamed, unexplored environment make many of us in the 20th century sometimes wish we could go back and feel the challenge along with them. For those who get such urges, there are still places to get satisfaction. The biggest classified wilderness area in the modern United States is only about a day's march west of the trails Colter blazed, and if he were to find himself there right now the only difference he'd find would be that the Blackfeet have stopped looking for him.

The wilderness covers nearly 1.3 million acres on both sides of the Bitterroot Mountains in Western Montana and Eastern Idaho. It is an area of unbelievable beauty extending into four different national forests that include lakes, streams, rivers and high mountain peaks. Parts of it are still unexplored and most of it is inaccessible except by canoe or on horseback, just as it was when it was one more obstacle in the path of the Lewis and Clark Expedition back in 1805.

It marks the eastern boundary of the Columbia Plateau and the Snake River Plain, a crescent that extends for 700 miles into the Cascade Mountains of Washington and points its tip in the direction of Mount Rainier, tallest, at 14,408 feet, of more than 100 impressive, symmetrical volcanic peaks extending down toward the Sierra Nevada Mountains of California. Rainier comes within 90 feet of being the tallest mountain on the United States mainland and it is easily a contender for consideration as the most beautiful mountain in the world. It rises up from the waters of Puget Sound on a base that covers some 100 square miles. It holds more than 25 glaciers on its sides, as well as meadows that contain more than 700 different species of wildflowers. As the altitude increases, so do climate conditions, and spring doesn't arrive at the summit until the calendar says it is nearly fall at the base. The result is a summer-long display of colorful flowers progressively moving up the mountain. Around the base is an equally impressive evergreen forest so dense it is never possible to see the mountain above. The Douglas firs, hemlocks and cedars form a roof that defies the sun, even when it does come out, which isn't very often in the Pacific Northwest. Moss covers everything, and the accumulation of fallen needles makes the ground cushiony soft, and in this particular corner of the American wilderness the whole world has turned to shades of green.

It's hard to imagine, with that green roof overhead, that there is a volcano up there. It's even harder when you're looking at the mountain from across the way in Seattle. But at one time Rainier was about 2,000 feet higher than it is today. An explosion much more devastating than the recently remembered one at nearby Mount Saint Helens blew its top off, leaving a jagged crater that was eventually filled in by other eruptions. The last was as recent as 1870.

One of the greatest volcanic explosions in the history of North America was also in the Cascades, though no one knows for sure when it happened. For all its apparent violence, it left us with one of the most beautiful natural wonders anywhere on the continent, a lake nearly 2,000 feet deep and 20 miles around where there was once a mountain 12,000 feet high. Oregon's Crater Lake has been called one of the most peaceful and beautiful sights anywhere in the world.

Anyone moving south through the Cascades toward Lassen Peak and the Sierra Nevada Mountains might find dozens of spots to challenge that statement, and when they get into the High Sierras they'll probably find dozens more. Because in this part of the American Wilderness, where the mountains are lush on the western slopes and dry on the east, the general feeling is like being on the edge of Paradise.

One of the first Europeans to see this wilderness arrived at the mouth of the Columbia River in April, 1825. Except for short journeys to London to tell the world of the wonders of the Western wilderness, he spent the next eight years wandering through the Pacific Northwest and California. In the process, he identified and named more than 200 different varieties of trees and plants, including the magnificent one that has his name, the Douglas fir.

David Douglas didn't fit the image of men like John Colter and Daniel Boone, who conquered the wilderness by becoming as rough as their environment. He had all the earmarks of a Scottish gentleman, and if they were making a movie of his life, a young Spencer Tracy could convincingly portray him. He arrived in North America as the official representative of the Horticultural Society of London, with letters of introduction to the officials of the Hudson's Bay Company and those among its employees who could read. The Society hadn't thought of preparing him for Indians, but he did have a good rifle and had learned back in the Scottish Highlands how to use it. On one of his first days of exploring, he stumbled on an Indian village where he was welcomed and entertained with an exhibition of fancy shooting. He quickly realized that the braves had never bothered to learn how to shoot a bird on the wing, a trick that was no trick at all back home. He casually tossed a rock at an eagle in the underbrush, and when it took flight he brought it down with a single shot. The Indians were impressed, but guessing it had been a lucky shot, one of them tossed a hat into the air. Douglas shot away all of the crown, leaving just the brim to flutter back to the ground. It earned him an instant reputation that stayed with him through all of his travels. But just in case his fame hadn't preceded him, he later said "it was of the utmost value to bring down a bird flying when going near the lodges, taking care to make it appear as if you were not observed." He heightened his image by using sunlight and a magnifying glass to light his pipe.

In his first two years of botanizing, he estimated that he covered more than 7,000 miles, most of it on foot. Then he decided to cross the Rocky Mountains. Five months later, he had traveled another 2,500 miles and was on a ship headed for home. By the time he got there, the seeds and specimens he had collected in the Northwest had already arrived. He had shipped far too many for the Horticultural Society's own gardens, and so the seeds were divided among the members, who planted them on their estates all over England.

He went back to North America again in 1830 and turned his eyes toward the mountains of California, which was part of the Mexican Republic in those days. It took him four months to prove he wasn't an Anglo spy and to get a temporary passport that would allow him to do his exploring. He used the time to learn Spanish.

His first trip into the wild gave him his first look at the giant redwood trees that had been discovered in the1780s by Archibald Menzies. Their beauty, he wrote, "plainly tells that we are not in Europe." He never saw the even bigger sequoia trees. But he found and classified hundreds of others and wrote to a friend, "You will begin to think I manufacture pines at my pleasure."

During his stay in California, the Horticultural Society had fallen on hard times back in London. They were having a problem collecting membership fees, and a published report noted that its delinquents included "one king, one duke, thirteen earls and twelve clergymen." Douglas was cut off without a sponsor and without funds. Interestingly, some of the roots and cones he sent back to them might have been the answer to their problems. They had flakes of gold attached to them. There was enough on one of them, Douglas said, "to make a watch seal." That was in 1831, eighteen years before gold was officially discovered in California. The British plant enthusiasts thought nothing of it, though some of them wished they had after the gold rush began. Douglas, meanwhile, also unimpressed by flakes of gold, went back north to the Columbia River as a free agent. On his way there he discovered a variety of white fir at the base of Mount Saint Helens. When he shipped its cones back to England, he enclosed a note that said, "A forest of these trees is a spectacle too much for one man to see."

Douglas went from the Northwest soon after to explore the Sandwich Islands, now known as Hawaii. He died a horrible death there in 1834, after having fallen into a concealed pit and being trampled by a bull for whom the pit had been dug as a trap. He was 35 years old.

During his two years in California, Douglas explored the Coast Range from his base on the Monterey Peninsula. He never roamed far enough into the interior to climb the Sierra Nevada Mountains. There were days he could see them from where he was, and he must have been curious about what grew there, especially after having seen the giant sequoias. But if he had seen the High Sierras from the east instead of the west, he would have found them irresistible. The mountains form a wall of rock rising two-and-a-half miles above sea level from the desert floor and extend 400 miles from north to south. Douglas would have loved it! As well as an explorer, he was also a noted mountain climber. He was the first white man to climb the Canadian Rockies, first to scale any of the Cascades and Oregon's Blue Mountains, and in his last days, he was first to climb the Hawaiian mountain peaks. The eastern side of the Sierras would have presented just the right challenge for a man like that to rise to. If he had, he may have wandered into the Inyo National Forest not far north of Death Valley and discovered the wonderful bristlecone pine, a tree that wasn't found until 1956, though some of the trees alive today have been living there for well over 4,000 years.

He missed a lot more than that. His fellow Scotsman, the naturalist John Muir, said that the forests of the Sierra Nevada are "the grandest and most beautiful in the world." But Douglas also missed the wonderful Yosemite Valley, the crown jewel of the High Sierras. Muir said it is a place with "the most songful streams in the world ... the loftiest granite domes, the deepest ice-sculptured canyons." The 1,189 square-mile Yosemite National Park is visited by more than two-and-a-half million people every year, who get some of the same feelings Douglas experienced when he visited the virgin wilderness to the north. It is a virtually unspoiled wilderness in a valley surrounded by sheer walls above which are alpine meadows, lakes and snowfields. The waterfalls are some of the country's most spectacular. The upper and lower Yosemite Falls, along with their cascades, are 2,425 feet high, second in the world only to Angel Falls in Venezuela.

When Douglas headed for California his goal wasn't to explore more pine forests, but to discover a new kind of wilderness along the Gila River. The Sonoran Desert he was headed for, one of five distinct desert regions in North America, extends from the lower part of Arizona some 250 miles below the Mexican border and includes nearly all of Baja California. Death Valley, which he surely would have seen if his plans had worked out, is actually part of the Mojave Desert, but the distinctions are vague. He certainly would have remembered it. It is the hottest place in the world, having established the all-time record back in 1913, when the temperature rose to 134.6 degrees. That was during the day of course. The mercury plunged to 93 degrees after the sun went down. It stayed that way for ten days, during which the daytime temperature averaged more than 125 degrees. What has the thermometer been up to lately? Nothing as spectacular as that, but a nearby weather station has, since weather records began to be saved, recorded temperatures above 90 degrees at least once each month for every month except December.

But Death Valley itself, in spite of that, does experience a winter season. What water there is freezes at least once every year. And every now and then the desert is covered with snow. No one who lives there has a collection of scarfs and mittens, but some old desert dwellers swear that some of the birds and animals hibernate to survive the winters. Whether that is true or not is open to question. You tend to hear a lot of tall tales from desert old-timers. But if they begin to tell you how the animals survive the summers, the first fact you may find hard to believe is that there is any wildlife in the desert at all. There is. But the reason why it is so hard to believe is that you don't see many signs of life out there. That's one of the ways they survive. They don't run around much in the noonday sun.

Jackrabbits are a good example. The desert is full of them, but as soon as the sun comes up in the morning, they lie down in the shade of the bushes and don't stir until the sun goes down again. Meanwhile, they keep cool by using their ears. That's no old-timer's yarn, either. Jackrabbits and other hares have unusually long ears, out of all proportion to the size of their bodies. The better to hear you with, you might say. But the real reason is that their ears serve as heat-dispersing organs. When the temperature of the air drops below the animal's body temperature, its ears radiate heat from its body. When it gets hotter, the rabbit cuts off the blood supply to the ears and no heat is absorbed. Other small mammals keep cool during the day by burrowing into the soft earth. Packrats are an exception, preferring to stay above ground or to hide in the shelter of rocks during the day. Either way, they air-condition their dens by collecting sticks and cactus branches which give off small amounts of moisture that evaporates and cools the pile of junk they've accumulated and carefully stacked to allow for good air circulation.

But the desert is best-served by the burrowing creatures like lizards and snakes. Their efforts to escape the heat of the day aerates the soil, and their presence provides nitrates for the roots of the plants trying to survive in the loose soil above.

Though it is teeming with life, the Southwestern desert came by its name when the Spanish arrived there in the 16th century and pronounced it "desierto," deserted. When English-speaking settlers began moving into the West, they saw the word on old maps and carefully avoided the place. The Mormons came and dug canals to make some of the desert bloom in their sense of the word. And the lure of riches from silver mines brought others, who convinced themselves that, once you get used to it, the heat isn't so terrible. Even today they'll tell you that there is no humidity in their environment and so the heat is inconsequential. But near cities like

Phoenix and Tucson, they've dug swimming pools and thrown fountains into the air. The trees and flowers they plant around their houses transpire water to keep cool. An ordinary apple tree sends some 2,000 gallons of water into the air through its leaves in a single season. The result is that, in making the desert bloom, they have built the humidity level to a point where many simply leave town during the hottest months. People can do that. And animals can get away from it all by retreating into tunnels. But the plants that make the American desert unique and beautiful are rooted to the spot, exposed to all the extremes of heat and cold, including the occasional snow and the summer cloudbursts.

Though it is the hottest and driest spot on the continent, Death Valley is home to more than 600 species of plants, nearly two dozen of which grow nowhere else. There are two kinds of orchids and close to a dozen different kinds of ferns. For the most part they get their moisture from deep beneath the surface where, under the right conditions, water from the occasional rainstorm can stay unevaporated for years. Mesquite and cottonwood trees often have roots 100 feet deep, which is why ranchers have so much trouble getting rid of them when they want to clear pastureland. Some plants have developed waxy coatings on their leaves to keep them from losing internal moisture. Others have hairlike coverings on their leaves to cut down the drying effects of the wind. Some curl their leaves to keep the sun from evaporating their water supply, and others drop their leaves in extremely dry times and replace them when moisture becomes more plentiful.

Nearly every desert plant survives by retaining moisture, saving it for a rainy day. And because they do, animals and birds survive as well. Desert quails have adapted to surving on less than a teaspoon of water a day, and they get every drop from the plants around them. Roadrunners are also non-drinkers, and race around the desert floor at an average of 20 miles an hour in the heat of the day. They get all the moisture they need from the food they eat, and there seems to be nothing they won't eat. They are as happy with a tarantula as with a June bug and, when all else fails, they'll eat the leaves from the trees. Most meat-eating mammals that live in the desert survive the same way, and will eat just about anything that is moist and moving. But coyotes, famous in movie cartoons as preferring roadrunners as the delicacy of choice, are the four-footed match of the cuckoo with the Americanized name. They will eat anything at all, as long as they can sink their teeth into it. A hungry coyote will be content with a good book until something better comes along. Very few desert creatures are selective about what they'll eat, but some, like squirrels and skunks, are basically vegetarians, preferring to dine at dawn, when the leaves are covered with dew. Like plants, desert animals also carry internal reservoirs in the form of fat, which turns to water when it is oxidized. Some birds and most reptiles carry water in their bodies, as do bighorn sheep, who consume more water than they need when they find a waterhole, which tides them over until the next time they find one.

Europeans have been exploring the deserts of Mexico and the American Southwest longer than any other part of North America, yet even today it is an unyielding wilderness in most places. One party of Spaniards who crossed the desert in1540 with their shiny helmets and Castilian armor catching the rays of the sun, had gone twenty days without a hint of water anywhere when suddenly they spotted a river. It was just about a mile away, but the mile was straight down. They had found the Grand Canyon, almost 70 years before Henry Hudson sailed into New York Bay, 80 years before the Pilgrims began to colonize New England … and 329 years before any white man dangled his feet in the white water they saw so far beneath their feet.

Though the Grand Canyon is a 1.2 million-acre national park visited by thousands every day, and though it is possible to drive a car over it or around it, it is still very much a part of the American wilderness. Some 220 species of birds are at home there with 67 different kinds of mammals, 27 species of reptiles and five species of amphibians. The South Rim, which is 6,900 feet high, is the most visited spot. The North Rim, about 18 miles across, is closed in winter because of the heavy snows. But most visitors never go over there because the trip is 215 miles long.

The national parks and national forests preserve much of the wilderness of North America for us and for our children, but places like the Grand Canyon and the Sonoran Desert have defied development. Even along the East Coast, where the idea of preservation came too late, nature has managed to reclaim what man has destroyed in many places and it is still possible to feel a little of what the original settlers found. But there is one part of Wilderness America that exists only in old photographs and occasional preserves, few of which are over a thousand acres. Yet not much more than a century ago, it covered more than a third of the Continental United States.

One of the first Europeans to see it was Louis Joliet, who explored the Mississippi River in 1673. His report of what he saw said, "A settler would not there spend ten years in cutting down and burning the trees. On the very day of his arrival he could put his plough into the ground." That is precisely what happened. And exactly why the American prairie no longer exists as part of the wilderness. Wheat and corn have replaced the tall grasses, and where buffalo once roamed cattle graze today. Most of it still feels the same as it did when Washington Irving said it gave him "the consciousness of being far beyond the bounds of human habitation."

When he was negotiating to buy the territory from France, Thomas Jefferson received a report that said the plains "have not had, and will not have, a single bush on them for ages." It was a strange landscape to people who had never experienced grasslands, and no one knew for sure how it got that way. Some said there were no trees on the prairie because the soil was no good. Others said that the herds of buffalo crushed any young trees that tried to take root. Many were convinced that any trees that tried to grow were killed off in the fires the Indians were forever setting to flush out game. There were several factors at work in creating the American grasslands. The soil is among the richest in the world. And the tall grass was growing long before buffalo began wandering through it and the Indians began setting fire to it. The landscape was originally carved by the great glaciers, which also left behind powdery soil that was distributed even further by the wind. It is wonderful soil for grasses. Trees thrive in it, too, but since it is thin, it doesn't hold as much moisture as trees need. A lot of it doesn't get much moisture in the first place. The prevailing weather pattern in North America is guided by streams of air moving from west to east. The winds that carry moisture from the Pacific Ocean lose their water as they pass over mountains, which force the flow upward to higher altitudes where the cooler air causes condensation. By the time the air mass has crossed the Rocky Mountains, it has also crossed the Pacific Coast Range, the Sierras and Cascades and it reaches the flat plains quite dry. The climate there is terrific for grasses, which took

over the landscape millions of years ago. As the plains roll eastward, moisture moving north from the Gulf of Mexico changes the character of the prairie, and near the Mississippi River the grass grows as tall as 20 feet, compared with an average of six inches back in Colorado. Why haven't trees adapted to life on the plains? Blame it on the grass. Many an early farmer discovered that the dense sod could more easily break a plow than be broken itself. The thick mat of grass uses every bit of the moisture within six or eight inches of the surface. When it rains, most of the water clings to the blades of grass and never reaches the soil, and when the sun shines almost none of it reaches the surface. And if all that isn't enough to doom any tree that tries to take root, the almost constant wind will break off its branches.

There are trees in the Plains States, of course. They grow on the eastern slopes of hillsides and in streambeds. Oaks and hickories, ashes, elms and cottonwoods thrive in many places. But it is the grasses that make the landscape in 15 states between the Mississipi River and the Rocky Mountains. And the sky. It seems to be without a limit. But it's not all waving grass and sunny sky. Though trees have a tough time competing with the grass, wildflowers get along very nicely and from May through October the colors march on as far as the eye can see. It begins before the snow has melted with the tender blue of the variety of anemone they call pasch flowers out on the prairie. Then come the white cat's-foot and windflowers, followed in a week or two by the biggest, purplest violets on the face of the earth. Before the spring sun has coaxed the grass out of the ground, the prairie is covered with Indian paintbrush, pinks and indigo. Wild strawberries and marsh marigolds add their colors to the spring show, which usually extends into June, when the wild roses, daylilies and daisies take center stage. And so it goes all summer long, changing every week or two with new flowers, new varieties. And all summer long the prairie is like a family reunion for daisies and their cousins, sunflowers, asters and the rest. You know the party is just about over when you can't touch the tops of the sunflowers even if you stand on tip-toes.

Where there are flowers, there are insects, of course, and when man first arrived on the prairie, almost a thousand different species of bees were already there. And almost no account of westward migration doesn't mention the millions of flies buzzing around in the grass. Where there is grass, you'll also find grasshoppers. In the late 19th century, settlers found that big grasshoppers often found them. They would come in swarms out of the west, eating everything that was green as they passed. One such cloud that took more than five hours to pass a given point was estimated to have been composed of about 125 billion hungry insects.

And where there are insects, there are also birds to eat them. The prairie is the hunting ground of hawks and owls, sparrows and doves. Meadowlarks are quite at home there, along with curlews and warblers. There are some 300 species of birds in that big sky over the center of the continent. And a little closer to the ground hundreds of kinds of butterflies. On the ground itself are gophers and squirrels and mice. They are the prey of coyotes, foxes, minks and weasels. And so it goes. Even though the grassy heart of America lost its wilderness status a century ago, many of the life forms that evolved out of it are still living out their days as though nothing happened.

It's the same story everywhere you go in America. Though man has protected some of the wilderness by legislation and restored some of what has been destroyed out of a sense of being part of the environment, nature herself is an old hand at changing and rechanging the world around us.

Americans are proud of their cities and their turnpikes and shopping malls that cover spaces the size of Manhattan Island. But the open spaces around them, even those that don't qualify as wilderness, are just as important to them. It's one reason why they spend so much time on those turnpikes. On an airline shuttle from Boston to Washington, flying over what may be the most heavily-populated corridor in the world, the view out the window is more often of fields, forests and seashores than of cities and subdivisions. The view from the observation deck on top of Chicago's Sears Tower is more of green than urban grid. And the short ride across the Golden Gate Bridge from San Francisco takes you to a virtually untouched area of hillsides and seacoast, parts of which could easily make you feel that no human being has ever walked there. Yet back there over your shoulder is one of the most dramatic panoramas ever created by man, the towers of the city.

When the first settlers arrived on the coast of North America from England, the thing that impressed them most was the density of the forests, an abundance of wood none of them had ever dreamed existed anywhere in the world. Exactly 300 years later, the British writer G.K. Chesterton followed in their footsteps and went home with the same impression. "I saw forests upon forests of small houses stretching away to the horizon as literal forests do," he wrote. "And they were, in another sense, literally like forests. They were all made of wood. It was almost as fantastic to an English eye as if they had been made of cardboard. The houses may look like a gypsy caravan on a heath or common, but they are not on a heath or common. They are on the most productive and prosperous land, perhaps, in the modern world. The wooden houses may fall down like shanties, but the fields would remain; and whoever tills those fields will count for a great deal in the affairs of humanity."

That was more than sixty years ago. The country has grown a great deal since then. More trees were cut, more houses built, more farmland cleared. But through it all some of the wilderness has, miraculously, come back to enrich us again.

Facing page: Devastation Trail in Hawaii Island's Volcanoes National Park.

Although it is only the third largest of the Hawaii's six islands, Oahu, which means "The Gathering Place," contains over 75% of Hawaii's people, half of whom live in Honolulu. This glamorous city, with its famous Waikiki Beach, attracts thousands of tourists each year, many of whom fail to explore the scenic delights of the rest of Oahu. The island's eastern backbone is the majestic, 37-mile-long Koolau Range. Where these mountains meet the windward coast they create a spectacular landscape of undulating folds and valleys (above). The island of Maui is distinguished by one of the finest of Hawaii's volcanic wonders, the spectacular Iao Needle (facing page). Green as an emerald, with its leafy covering,

the 2,250-foot-high needle rises sharply from the floor of a deep valley whose beauty belies its role as the site of a gruesome, but significant, event. For it was here, in 1790, that King Kamehameha I trapped and defeated the Maui army. Corpses choked the Iao Stream that cuts through the gorge and the battle was named Kepaniwai, meaning "the damming of the waters." Overleaf: among the splendors of Hawaii Island, the largest of the archipelago, are (left) the dramatic Na Ulu Sea Arches and (right) the vast crater of Kilauea Iki, in Volcanoes National Park. This great volcano last erupted in 1959 and even today molten lava still bubbles beneath its surface.

Previous pages: among the sensuous images associated with Hawaii Island are the brilliant colors of rare and beautiful flowers, each with its own heady fragrance. Sometimes called Orchid Island, it boasts over 20,000 varieties of orchids, as well as richly colored anthuriums (left) and delicate water hyacinth (right). Giant ferns, bamboo, azaleas and orchids flourish in the lush gorge of Akaka Falls State Park (above), which is one of the many attractions near Hilo on the island's northeast coast. The

Kolekole Stream runs through this 66-acre arboretum, dropping 442 feet over a mossy precipice to form the beautiful Akaka Falls (facing page). Mark Twain is quoted as having called the Waimea Canyon (overleaf) the "Grand Canyon of the Pacific." Although it may not match the size of Arizona's famous gorge, this canyon, on the island of Kauai, displays colors and shapes of equal splendor.

Previous pages: an Alp-like river gorge near Valdez, which is known as the "Switzerland of Alaska." Facing page: (top) one of the spectacular tidewater glaciers, and (bottom) Muir Inlet in Glacier Bay National Park. Below: Ruth Glacier, which relentlessly carves and shatters its path down the slopes of Mount McKinley (bottom). This awe-inspiring massif, overshadowing the Susitna River (right), dominates the other peaks in the Alaska Range and was known by the Indians as "Denali," or the "Great One." One of the state's prime attractions is the fantastic Mendenhall Glacier (overleaf), a creeping blanket of ice fed by the 4,000-square-mile Juneau Icefield.

Washington State boasts two of America's finest national parks. One is Olympic National Park, which embraces the great Olympic Mountains. Blanketing the southwest slopes of this range are dense coniferous forests containing such botanical delights as the Hall of Mosses (above), on the upper Hoh River, where gnarled trees dripping with velvety mosses rise from the ferny forest floor. In Mount Rainier National Park, a sparkling wonderland of glaciers is to be found on the broad dome of Mount Rainier (facing page), the highest volcanic peak in the Cascade Range. In lush, rain-soaked valleys around the base of the mountain grow cathedral-like forests of Western red cedar, Douglas fir, and other trees indigenous to the northwestern states.

Left: Falls Creek tumbling through Mount Rainier National Park, (below) the Rain Forest in Olympic National Park, and (bottom and overleaf) smooth Picture Lake backed by Mount Shuksan. Facing page: (top) the Palouse River winds through the canyons of eastern Washington, and (bottom) the snow-capped volcano, Mount St. Helens, rises above Spirit Lake.

Facing page: among the scenic splendors of Oregon's Pacific shores are the dramatic rock formations (top) of Harris Beach State Park and the rugged coves and bays (bottom) of the coastline south of Cannon Beach. Inland, one of the state's best known landmarks is Crater Lake, with its wildly beautiful surroundings (below) and the conical Wizard Island that seems to float on its smooth surface (bottom). Lying within the caldera of Mount Mazama, a collapsed volcano, it is one of the world's deepest lakes. Right: the lichen-covered Oneonta Gorge.

Top: South Falls in Silver Falls State Park, and (above) the Snake River carving its path through the black walls of Hells Canyon, one of the world's deepest river gorges. The Columbia River has also given Oregon a spectacular gorge. Here, cascading over lush cliffs, are a multitude of waterfalls, including the Wahkeena Falls (left) and the Multnomah Falls (overleaf right), which makes a 620-foot-drop in two steps and is the second highest waterfall in America. Facing page: (top) Warm Springs River, and (bottom) the Sahalie Falls. Overleaf left: (top) Crater Lake, and (bottom) the fast-flowing South Umpqua River, which has curious pillars of volcanic rock rising from its banks.

California boasts six of America's finest national parks, one of which, Redwood National Park (these pages), preserves the tallest trees known to man. Although coast redwoods can grow in several areas throughout the world it is only along this part of the Pacific coast that they reach such great heights. Facing page: redwoods soar skywards and (above) golden light outlines a moss-coated sapling at the base of its mother tree in Lady Bird Johnson Grove, which was named after the wife of President Lyndon B. Johnson. It was he who, in 1968, signed the park into being, making it one of the first institutions to protect trees from the voracious logging industry that boomed during the 1950s and early '60s.

Lassen Volcanic Park consists of 106,000 acres of California's most varied and fascinating terrain. There are coniferous forests, numerous lakes and mountains and, of course, much evidence of volcanic activity. Lofty Lassen Peak, which is reflected in Manzanita Lake (previous pages), dominates the park and was considered to be a dormant volcano until May 30, 1914. That was the day when, completely without warning, it erupted, sending rivers of red lava down its slopes and clouds of sulphuric ash high into the sky. Minor eruptions continued until 1921, since when it has been, once again, asleep. These pages: pine trees and golden aspens color the park. Seen from Tunnel View, the great, rectangular bulk of El Capitan faces the rounded peaks of Cathedral Rocks in Yosemite Valley (overleaf), the jewel of Yosemite National Park. The haunting beauty of this area was first made known to the public by journalists and writers in 1851, before which time it had been a secret, fiercely guarded by its inhabitants the Ahwahneechee Indians.

Previous pages: the view south from Hanging Rock (right) reveals the densely-forested valleys and sculptured mountains of Sequoia National Park extending to the horizon, while from Moro Rock, another of the park's splendid vantage points, can be seen the majestic peaks of Castle Rocks (left), which reach a height of 9,180 feet. Top: lush vegetation and huge granite boulders in the vicinity of the aptly-named Mirror Lake (facing page bottom), and (facing page top) the sunlit north face of Half Dome, all in Yosemite National Park. East of this region lies ancient Mono Lake (above), which is the oldest continuously-existing body of water in America and is noted for the strange calcified rock formations, called tufa, that rise from its shores. Overleaf: diffused sunlight in the mist-shrouded forest of Del Norte Coast Redwoods State Park, in Redwood National Park.

Top: Zabriskie Point, an area of 5-10 million-year-old lake beds in the rugged Black Mountains of Death Valley National Monument. Covering nearly two million acres, this great desert is one of the driest areas on earth and contains the lowest point in the western hemispere, 282 feet below sea level. It is not, however, as barren and "deathly" as it may seem, for the monument supports over 600 types of plants and roughly 230 species of bird life. Above right: cactii in the Living Desert Reserve, in Palm Desert, near Palm Springs, Southern California. Among Northern California's prime scenic attractions are 14,162-foot-high Mount Shasta, which overlooks boulder-strewn Gumboot Creek (above left), beautiful Emerald Bay (facing page), an inlet on the famous Lake Tahoe, and (overleaf) the 129-foot-high Burney Falls, near Burney.

Some of America's wildest landscapes are to be found in Wyoming. Flat Top Mountain (right) provides an unusual backdrop for Lower Green Lake in the Bridger Wilderness, while in Yellowstone National Park, hot water shoots up from the crater of Castle Geyser (above), and the Yellowstone River, seen from Artist Point, cascades in a silver torrent over the Lower Falls (facing page). The majestic Grand Teton Range towers above coniferous forests (top) and the serene Jackson Lake (overleaf) in Grand Teton National Park.

Previous pages: (left top) the sheer face of Garden Wall, towering above McDonald Creek, in Glacier National Park, (right top) the silver waters of the Gibbon River thread through lush grasslands in Yellowstone National Park, and in Grand Teton National Park, the Snake River (left bottom) curves through forests of pine, spruce and fir and the great Grand Teton peaks overlook the snow-covered sagebrush flats at Jackson Hole

(right bottom). The great wilderness areas of the Plains States are distinguished by many dramatic rock formations, including the eyecatching Chimney Rock (top), southeast of Scotts Bluff in Nebraska, the Chalk Pyramids (above left), at Monument Rocks in Kansas, and the strange peaks and ridges at the Pinnacles Overlook (above) and River Valley Cedar Pass (facing page) in South Dakota's Badlands National Park.

The majestic Rocky Mountains (these pages) stretch far beyond the boundaries of Colorado, but it is in this state that they are considered by many to be most picturesque. For here, their peaks caress clear, blue skies, while myriad rivers, lakes and streams sparkle below in valleys of conifers and golden aspen.

Facing page: sunset at Lodore Canyon. Carved by the incessant flow of the meandering Green River, the walls of this great gorge rise to a height of 3,300 feet. Above: shaded by brilliantly-colored autumn trees, Crystal Creek, in Gunnison National Forest, shimmers in the light of a cloudless Colorado sky.

Tranquil blue lakes (above) and golden aspens (left) constitute the breathtaking scenery of Rocky Mountain National Park, and in White River National Forest, Maroon Creek (top) snakes its way towards Aspen, jagged mountains overlook fish-filled Maroon Lake (facing page top) and foliage colors the land around Independence Pass (facing page bottom). Overleaf: Crystal Creek in Gunnison National Forest.

Much of Utah's wilderness, with its incredible sandstone formations, is protected in national parks, such as Capitol Reef (below) and Canyonlands (bottom). Arches National Park contains the massive, buttress-like spans of Double Arch (right) and the beautiful Delicate Arch (facing page top). Overlooking the waters of North Fork of the Virgin River is the Sentinel (facing page bottom), part of Zion National Park's spectacular Zion Canyon. Overleaf: a view from Inspiration Point of Bryce Canyon National Park.

America's most celebrated wilderness area is undoubtedly the Grand Canyon. This great gash in the earth runs for 300 miles, is almost a dozen miles wide and one mile deep. Its formation was largely due to the swift-flowing Colorado River (above right), which, some 25 million years ago, began to scour the flat plateau, cutting through layer after layer of rock. Above left: a bird's eye view of the Colorado River from the Point Sublime area, and (top) late evening light lends warm colors and long shadows to the canyon as seen from Mohave Point on the South Rim. Facing page: (top) from Mather Point Lookout the layered rock strata unfold to a level horizon, shaded by buff grays, delicate mauves and light golds, and (bottom) sunset from Desert View Lookout. Overleaf: (left top) the lush oasis of Havasu Falls, (left bottom) the dramatically-lit Battleship, viewed from Pima Point, and (right top and bottom) the changing light of day alters views of the canyon below West Rim Drive.

The 200-foot-high El Morro National Monument in New Mexico is also known as "Inscription Rock," due to the ancient Indian petroglyphs that are carved into its soft sandstone. Arizona's Petrified Forest National Park takes its name from the many, 160-million-year-old, petrified logs that lie scattered over its strange, moon-like landscape. This setting has its own fascinating features, including the eroded layered rock deposits of the Flattops (above) and the banded, cone-shaped hills of Blue Mesa (right). Pine, juniper and cypress trees surround the huge and colorful sentinels of Cathedral Rock (facing page top and overleaf) in Oak Creek Canyon, near Sedona, and the extraordinary buttes (facing page bottom) create a fantasy-like scene at Monument Valley Navajo Tribal Park.

In Oak Creek Canyon (top), splashes of green foliage bring a refreshing contrast to the neutral tones that characterize much of Arizona's rocky land. This lovely canyon is one of a series of steep-walled gorges dissecting the southern margin of the Colorado Plateau. The Granite Dells (above), near Prescott, is a popular summer playground area comprising curiously-formed granite rocks reflected in beautiful, glassy lakes. The several thousand square miles that constitute Monument Valley

Navajo Tribal Park lie within the reservation of the Navajo Indians, who have clothed the park's great, isolated sandstone towers in rich mythology. Several towers, such as West Mitten, East Mitten and Merrick Butte (facing page top), stand as high as 1,000 feet above the red valley floor. To the north of Petrified Forest National Park is the remarkable Painted Desert (facing page bottom), which was so named by Spanish explorers due to the bands of brilliant color in its sculptured rock.

Previous pages: (left top) Inks Lake, one of a series of highland lakes on the lower Colorado River, in Texas, (right) the steep cliffs of Santa Elena Canyon near Kingsland, and (left bottom) the peak of El Capitan in Guadalupe Mountains National Park. The distinctive Guadalupe Mountains (above right) were formed millions of years ago beneath an inland sea as part of the Capitan Reef. Facing page: (top) Caddo Lake State Park, near Jefferson, where, in a maze of channels and bayous on Lake Caddo, are cypress groves laden with Spanish moss, and (bottom) the Palo

Duro Canyon, which was carved by the Prairie Dog Town Fork of the Red River. Above left: a meadow of brilliant red Indian paintbrush and Texas bluebonnets, the official State Flower, (top right) sunset over the 640-acre forest on the eastern shoreline of Lake Livingston, in Lake Livingston State Park, and (top left) the Rio Grande, which forms Texas' boundary with Mexico, at Hot Springs, in Big Bend National Park, a vast park covering 708,118 acres with some of the wildest desert in America.

Time seems to have stood quite still for the peaceful towns, small farms and family homesteads in the Ozarks. This 200-square-mile section of northern Arkansas and southern Missouri is a place where 19th-century rural America is really evoked. It is also an area of great natural beauty, with rolling, forested hills surrounded by prairies, intersected by grassy valleys, undermined with natural caves and deep springs, and laced with rapid crystal streams. Attractions in the Missouri section include (left) the incredible formations of the Meramec Caverns near Stanton, (below) Alley Spring, in Shannon County, and (facing page top) sun-dappled Round Spring which, despite its calm appearance, has a daily flow of 26,000,000 gallons of water. Piney Creek (bottom left), near Pelsor and the Little Missouri Falls (facing page bottom) in Montgomery County are two of the scenic waterways in the Arkansas Ozarks.

Above: the Mississippi River near the Missouri town of Hannibal, which is famous as the birthplace of Samuel Clemens, later to become Mark Twain, one of the most celebrated authors in American history. His childhood experiences in this beautiful region, by the curving banks of the Mississippi, in the lush woods and exciting caves, provided inspiration for the great stories of Tom Sawyer and Huckleberry Finn. Table Rock State Park (facing page) is one of Missouri's finest recreational areas and consists of 456 acres of densely-wooded land on the northeast shores of Table Rock

Lake. Overleaf: the lower Mississippi River loops and twists over the land in a manner that led Mark Twain to describe its shape as "a long, pliant apple-paring." Strange swampy backwaters are the result of these meanderings and they can often be exceptionally beautiful. Coahoma County (left bottom) in the state of Mississippi boasts the lovely DeSoto Lake (right bottom and left top), the mirror-like surface of which reflects the ribbed and fluted tree-trunks that pierce its waters. In Washington County is Leroy Percy State Park (right top), where menacing alligators lurk in the shadowy swamp.

The Deep-South state of Alabama encompasses a great variety of landscapes, stretching from a mountainous northern region, across forest-clad hills and verdant lowlands, to its almost tropical Gulf Coast. Near Hodges, in the northwest, is the much-prized beauty spot of Rock Bridge Canyon (top and facing page), where great rock formations, some shot through with veins of quartz and some splashed by waterfalls, are set in groves of fern, mountain laurel, magnolia and azalea. Above and overleaf: a solitary bird stands guard over the waters near Fort Morgan on the picturesque Gulf Coast. This area is actually part of Pleasure Island, which used to be a peninsula until the Intra-Coastal Waterway Canal separated it from the mainland. Today, the aptly-named island provides Alabama with a luxurious, thirty-mile stretch of recreational seashore, comprising lush vegetation and white, sandy beaches all lapped by the warm waves of the Gulf of Mexico.

In Southern Florida, a fifty-mile-wide, hundred-mile-long river flows, slowly and almost imperceptibly, from Lake Okeechobee to Florida Bay. It creates the Everglades, a subtropical wilderness of such beauty and variety, and so rich in rare plant and animal life, that it has no equal. Man continues to make developments here - Flamingo was once a small fishing settlement but is now a tourist center for Everglades National Park - but nature also initiates change - the old road to Flamingo (left), now traveled only on foot, is being fast encroached upon by the surrounding forest. Below: sunset over a prairieland of sawgrass and dwarf cypresses. Bottom: epiphyte, or air plants, growing on wild pine. These non-parasitic epiphytes use trees purely for support, in order to avoid the inhospitable extremes of wet or dry that exist at ground level in the Everglades. Overleaf: sunrise beyond a stand of slash pines.

Top: a view from the Richard Russell Scenic Highway of the rolling, green-mantled mountains of northern Georgia. This spectacular route runs for fourteen miles, curving around glassy lakes, passing miles of untouched forest and reaching elevations ranging from 1,600 to 3,000 feet. Almost a century ago a process of erosion began to eat into the chalk, blue marl and red clay that color the great fissure (above and facing page top) of Georgia's "Little Grand Canyon," or Providence Canyon State Park, near Columbus. Facing page bottom: swamplands around Agrirama, near Tifton. Overleaf: (left) the skeletons of dead trees rise from a green forest floor in Great Smoky Mountain National Park, Tennessee, and (right) Cypress Gardens, north of Charleston in South Carolina, a 160-acre wonderland containing azaleas, cypress trees, and camellias.

Except for the Pacific Northwest, nowhere in America gets more rainfall than the section of the southern Appalachian Chain known as the Great Smoky Mountains. Here, providing Tennessee with some of its finest scenery, are lush forests, rushing streams, and waterfalls, such as the Rainbow Falls (left) near Cherokee Orchard. Above: a misty valley in the Smoky Mountains viewed from Morton Overlook, (top) sunset over Pickwick Lake at Pickwick Landing, near Savannah, and (facing page) the silver cascade of Fall Creek Falls, east of Spencer.

Previous pages: (right) the Northrap Falls in Colditz Cove Natural Area, one of Tennessee's major attractions, and (left) sunset over the wooded highlands of western North Carolina, seen from the Blue Ridge Parkway. This famous scenic drive follows the Appalachian Chain for 469 miles, passing through its many parallel ranges, with their cloud-filled valleys and endless forests. The route begins in Virginia's Shenandoah National Park and, south of Asheville, begins to offer views of that part of Great Smoky Mountains National Park located in North Carolina (facing page top). Where the drive ends, at the park entrance near Cherokee, another road continues, leading into the heart of the park, to the crest of the Great Smokies at Newfound Gap. Located on the Tennessee/North Carolina border, the gap affords fine panoramas (facing page bottom) from a height of 5,048 feet. Top right: Rock Bridge, one of about twenty natural stone arches in the remarkable Red River Gorge of Daniel Boone National Forest, and (top left) a cornfield near Barbourville, in the valley of the scenic Cumberland River (above), in Kentucky.

Previous pages: the delicate cascades of Burgess Falls, in Burgess Falls State Natural Area near Sparta, Tennessee. Seashore State Park near Cape Henry in Virginia is a naturalists' paradise. Within its 2,700 acres of lakes, bays and inland waterways are to be found over 336 species of plants and trees, ranging fron giant yuccas to bald cypress trees festooned with Spanish moss (facing page and above). Top: the waters of Chagrin Falls, just east of Cleveland, Ohio, (left) winter snow on Amnicon Falls State Park, near Superior in Wisconsin, and (overleaf) the Gooseberry River, one of Minnesota's many scenic waterways.

The five Great Lakes: Superior, Michigan, Huron, Erie and Ontario, support a rich variety of flora and fauna and provide some mid-west states with superb scenic attractions. Along the shores of Lake Michigan in western Michigan are to be found the golden sand dunes (above and left) of Warren Dunes State Park, south of Benton Harbor, and (top) the marshland near Whitehall by the White Lake. The Gooseberry River (facing page) curves gracefully through the 638 acres of Gooseberry State Park and forms one of Minnesota's finest beauty spots where it cascades for 240 feet into Lake Superior.

Not only does Minnesota (these pages) have Lake Superior as part of its eastern boundary but also contains myriad lakes and inland waters that cover an area of some 5,000 square miles. Island Lake (previous pages) in Becker County, Minnesota, overflows its bounds, drowning parts of the surrounding forest and creating a strange, swampy wilderness. To many minds the finest Lake Superior scenery is at Grand Marais (above), which each year attracts artists eager to capture the subtle coloration and dramatic forms of its coastal rocks and the excitement of the sea crashing against them. Grand Marais falls within the 3,000,000 acres of Superior National Forest, a magnificent wilderness clothed in forests of spruce and pine and perforated by a system of beautiful lakes and streams. Further along the shores of Lake Superior, near Silver Bay, is Beaver Bay, into which Beaver Creek (facing page) swiftly flows, tumbling and cascading through woodland on its way.

Not only can New York State lay claim to what is probably the most famous city on the continent, but also to some of the most exciting and varied scenery, ranging from the thunderous splendor of Niagara Falls to the quiet beauty of the Thousand Islands in the St. Lawrence River. Previous pages: among the state's loveliest recreational areas are Catskill Park (right), which boasts all the misty, haunted beauty of the Catskill Mountains less than 100 miles from New York City, and Montour Falls (left), the southern gateway to the Finger Lakes Region. Situated by Cayuga Lake, one of these six long Finger Lakes, is Taughannock Falls State Park (these pages), site of the magnificent 215-foot-high Taughannock Falls (facing page).

The northeastern corner of New York State is distinguished by what are thought to be the oldest mountains in the world, the Adirondacks. At one time they were taller than the Rockies and their highest peak, the famous Whiteface Mountain (previous pages right) reaches an impressive elevation of 5,344 feet. On the way to this mountain's summit, along Route 86, beautiful scenery may be enjoyed as the road winds through breathtaking countryside and past gushing mountain waters (previous pages left). The main commercial center of this region is Plattsburgh, situated on a bay (above) in the glittering Lake Champlain. South of here is the mouth of the Salmon River (facing page), which has its source in the Silver Lake Mountains. Overleaf: the varied and colorful woodland on the slopes of the Adirondack Mountains beside the beautiful 32-mile-long Lake George.

Lying off the rocky coast of Maine, Mount Desert Island has a wild charm and remoteness that has long attracted vacationers, artists and nature lovers. The concern of islanders and summer visitors alike that it should not be subject to overdevelopment led to the formation, in 1919, of Acadia National Park, which to this day protects the island's quiet forests, dramatic mountains and idyllic coastline. Above: leaves of russet, gold and lime green against a brilliant blue sky over a park in Bar Harbor, the commercial center of Mount Desert Island and a base for visitors to the park, and (facing page) boulders along the island's southeastern shoreline. New England is at its most spectacular during the fall, when, as if touched by the brush of an artist, the cool green shades of summer give way to brilliant tones of copper, brown and gold. At this time hundreds of wide-eyed tourists flock to scenic areas such as Crawford Notch State Park (overleaf), New Hampshire, to witness nature's annual miracle.

The White Mountains of the Appalachian Chain, cut by their scenic valleys, or notches, and overlooking cascading streams and sky-blue lakes, have given New Hampshire a wilderness area of incredible appeal. Within the thousand square miles of White Mountain National Forest are such features as Mount Washington, which is one of the highest mountains in America and stands with other great peaks in the majestic Presidential Range. The eastern valley of this range is Pinkham Notch, which offers such scenic delights as the spectacular rushing waters (above) of Glen Ellis Falls, which has a 65-foot drop and ranks among the state's highest waterfalls. Another interesting part of the forest is Rocky Gorge Scenic Area, a great ravine pitted with hundreds of potholes and washed by the rapid Swift River (facing page) plunging into it from a height of 20 feet. Overleaf: great boulders in the froth and bubble of the Swift River near Conway.

Vermont's fall has become something of an institution. From early September to mid-October reports on color progress are issued weekly, foliage counts are taken and festivals are held to celebrate this fantastic season. As the weeks progress, birches, witch hazels and elms turn bright yellow and gold, and ivy trees, ashes, sumacs and red maples give hues ranging from deep crimson to warm vermilion, while the fiery oranges are those of the sugar maple (above). This species also gives Vermont its most famous export, maple syrup, which is first extracted as sap from the tree trunks and then reduced in sugar houses. Overleaf: the fall colors of New Hampshire at White Mountain National Forest (left top and bottom), seen from Sugar Hill Lookout (right top), and the Ellis River Valley (right bottom).

Facing page top: snow scattered over New Hampshire's White Mountain scenery, where the Saco River flows through the red-spruce-dotted woodland of Crawford Notch State Park (top). Facing page bottom: Bear Brook overlooked by the stony face of The Gorge, in the Cadillac Mountain area of Mount Desert Island, Maine. Above: late afternoon light filters through trees near the coast at Old Saybrook, where the Connecticut River empties into Long Island Sound, in Connecticut, and (right) late autumn trees reflected in a glassy pond near Jeffersonville in Vermont.

Facing page: a woodland scene near Saint Albans, which is located close to one of America's most attractive stretches of water, the 107-mile-long Lake Champlain. The lake forms nearly half of the western boundary of Vermont and is named after the explorer who discovered it in 1609, Samuel de Champlain. Right: swampy land on the shores of Lake Champlain. Top: the gentle beauty of the sand dunes on Cape Cod, in Massachusetts, New England's beloved summer playground. Above: a ford near Old Mistick Village, a recreated 19th-century shopping village in Connecticut. Overleaf: Green Mountain scenery in Vermont, and (following page) Cascade Brook in Franconia Notch, the great, deep valley between the Franconia and Kinsman mountain ranges in New Hampshire.